EVERY MINUTE IS FIRST

EVERY MINUTE IS FIRST

IS FIRST

SELECTED LATE POEMS

MARIE-CLAIRE BANCQUART

TRANSLATED FROM THE FRENCH

BY JODY GLADDING

MILKWEED EDITIONS

This work received support for excellence in publication and translation from Albertine Translation, formerly French Voices, a program created by Villa Albertine.

Published 2024 by Milkweed Editions
Printed in Canada
Cover design by Mary Austin Speaker
Cover art: "Zinnias" by Susan Jane Walp
Author photo of Jody Gladding by David Hinton; author photo of Marie-Claire Bancquart by Adrienne Arth

24 25 26 27 28 5 4 3 2 1
First Edition

Library of Congress Cataloging-in-Publication Data

Names: Bancquart, Marie-Claire, author. | Gladding, Jody, 1955- translator.

Title: Every minute is first : selected and late poems of Marie-Claire Bancquart / translated from the French by Jody Gladding.
Description: Minneapolis : Milkweed Editions, 2024. | Summary: "The first full-length English translation of this celebrated French writer of the twentieth century, a penetrating and encompassing collection of her last works touching on death, domesticity, nature, language itself, and-always-the body"-- Provided by publisher.
Identifiers: LCCN 2023030172 (print) | LCCN 2023030173 (ebook) | ISBN 9781639550906 (trade paperback) | ISBN 9781639550913 (ebook)
Subjects: LCSH: Bancquart, Marie-Claire--Translations into English. | LCGFT: Poetry.
Classification: LCC PQ2662.A49 E94 2024 (print) | LCC PQ2662.A49 (ebook)
   | DDC 841/.914--dc23/eng/20230821
LC record available at https://lccn.loc.gov/2023030172
LC ebook record available at https://lccn.loc.gov/2023030173

Milkweed Editions is committed to ecological stewardship. We strive to align our book production practices with this principle, and to reduce the impact of our operations in the environment. We are a member of the Green Press Initiative, a nonprofit coalition of publishers, manufacturers, and authors working to protect the world's endangered forests and conserve natural resources. *Every Minute Is First* was printed on acid-free 100% postconsumer-waste paper by Friesens Corporation.

CONTENTS

PREFACE

On tient toujours le bout du monde, n'importe où.
Il ne refuse pas
d'être rompu comme un pain tendre.

We're always holding the end of the world, no matter where.
It doesn't refuse
to be broken like fresh bread.

How accurately Marie-Claire Bancquart transcribes, in this short poem, our shaky grasp on a fragile planet that, breaking, nevertheless sustains us—cause for suffering or celebration? As sign of life *and* danger, this tremor pervades the collection. Bodies of water, beloved pets, cities are all traversed by it, so that a kind of leveling occurs, and the realm of animate, sentient beings opens to include, companionably, the dead and the living, the tree and the stone, the contents of a kitchen drawer and the fallen empire. And words. Bruised words clamoring to be let in, words the poet works like dough or approaches gently as a lover, words "become sun and place."

Marie-Claire Bancquart was born in 1932 and lived in Paris for most of her life. For much of her childhood, she suffered from tuberculosis that affected her spine and confined her to a hospital bed. That confinement was formative. Unable to attend school, she became an avid reader at an early age and was particularly attuned to the smallest sensations, the physical body. She began writing poetry at fifteen or sixteen.

Based on her childhood experiences, her first novel, *Le temps immobile*, was published in 1960. She continued to publish poetry, novels, short stories, and literary criticism for the next sixty years. She and her husband, the musician and composer Alain Bancquart, whom she met as a university student in 1955, collaborated on many projects and toured throughout the world presenting their work. Bancquart taught French literature at the Sorbonne until her retirement in 1994. She died in 2019.

If the poems in this collection register ever more keenly the trembling that shakes us into awareness, it's because they are *late* poems. Bancquart was particularly prolific in her final years, producing eight volumes of poetry between 2005 and 2018. Yet the work itself becomes increasingly spare as death approaches and the poet takes stock of a "provisional," "ambiguous" life. In accurate, concise, and stripped-down language, the poem serves as journal for the passing days and the practice of living—lightly—in the present on this planet.

Toute minute est première was originally published in France in 2019. The poems were selected from Bancquart's last eight books by Claude Ber with the approval of the poet, who died while the book was in production. Claude Ber then added a group of final unpublished poems. This English translation includes roughly two-thirds of the original volume and represents Bancquart's work at its most accomplished. I'm deeply grateful to Claude Ber for her initial astute selection and her excellent preface in the French edition. Deep thanks as well to Richard Begault of Le Castor Astral and Daniel Slager of Milkweed Editions for bringing Bancquart's poems to French- and English-language readers, and to the Albertine Translation fund for supporting this project.

I first fell in love with Bancquart's poetry when I came upon it in an anthology twenty-five years ago. Translating this late work has revealed to me its endless surprises, sense of humor, and fealty to language itself. My deepest gratitude to Marie-Claire Bancquart for making poems that take on a life of their own.

JODY GLADDING

EVERY MINUTE IS FIRST

OTHER

As if I were
other than this hollowed moving thing

as if I were
other than this beautiful worn-out civilization, my own
with the taste of vainly agitated verbs
with the memory-future of gigantic ruins
and of other civilizations, dead mothers.

Between unity and nullity
nevertheless I live
a tightrope artist.

It's our shared home.

Not very habitable?

But the only one
allotted us.

IN

I'm in a fox's burrow
head curled over belly

I'm one word
nestled in another, like
lit in *délice, lent* in *calendrier*

the same way
the sea advances
the wind
refreshes the vines

but not like
missiles pollution rape.

Even so the Eiffel Tower
sparkles
ten minutes each hour, every night.

With it
a kind of joy.

ON THE BRINK OF LIFE

The dead need no more space than
between a mouth and its lipstick.

They skate across the shutters.

This slit of daylight
is their last look, spying on us
exchanging a kiss
in a moment of forgetting them.

They have thinned the wall
bored an opening
opposite the door.

Breeze
that rustles fabrics,

condensation on the mirror,

their breath from beyond-destiny.

Attentive   now   we wait.
We are
on the brink of things.

YES, THE INTERVAL

You think you can
shed the interval?

Woven with your body
you wouldn't be able to extract
a single fiber
without
unraveling yourself like a sock.

The adhesion
exists, it's strange:

you are one with that thin, fundamental gap
approaching
the beginning of the abyss
and
the beginning of joy.

EARTH

To spell a word whispered by our capillaries

to track
the blood that pulses in our wrists

to love the expansion of veins

clandestine
participation
in our long journey:

laid end to end
all our blood vessels
circle the earth two times.

Earth,
your insects, your flowers, your divinities,
have you arranged them along these routes?

OUT OF SCALE

Tiny boxwood leaf. A little rain on it:

its veins
enlarged

projected out of scale.

On the surface of the drop
our house distended
in the magic mirror

along the minuscule
edge
you're walking.

A world impossible and real
stuck with the leaf
on the lip of a statue.

She smiles
knowing
what separates her from us
forever.

FORWARD

From the background fog of sleep
some will never see a child coming forward.

They sleep only with themselves
and encounter each other in the night
adults
knowing that side of earth is closed to them:
cheeks smeared with blackberries
dreams of high seas conquered by pirates.

Their once upon a time is a concentration camp, a sickbed.

They turned from it

they are searching for
herbs to embalm its memory
a tomb for locking it away without libations

finally to walk forth, into the innocence of grass.

FALTERS, WEARS OUT

Go change.

But what if it wasn't your clothes, but yourself?

Go change.

What face will you choose?

So as not to abandon
your various pairs of hands
you put them in a suitcase to go through customs
you declare them as casts, copies.

But the heart, lungs, the secret
of what beats and thumps?
You were obliged to hide the spares so well
you lost them.

This body, which you wear all the time, falters, wears out.
Your new hands finger it, your mouth smiles, but nevertheless,
there it is: old.

GRASS BETWEEN THE LIPS

A blade of grass between the lips
produces a primitive sound
carried off by the wind.

We would like to seize it
to set it before us
like an accumulation of life's silences
perhaps finally sounding

but it
will escape us:

dense non-speech

that is not nothing, rather its opposite

and lies in wait
for another space where the contradiction might be lifted.

Pulsating
between these lips
that can't detain you,
goodbye.

ALONE

Tap, tap on your little
life slicker.

Dust of words released
pelting down on you
getting inhaled
reaching your very fingertips

tap, the computer
even counts
the number of letters.

And you
you wander about in your veins
you climb
your thoracic cage.

You are alone

the words have only passed through.

The body limp. Slobber, come.

The body hard. Its skeleton, its calluses.
Mute.

THIS DARK TREE

Book,
this dark tree, where the word
offers who knows what among the leaves:
poison, potion, balm?

Outside it's raining. The path has disappeared.

The embrace of things and the dead remains
whispering the adventure
of our unknowing.

Fog
envelops our clumsy exorcism
like wool.

And yet, an insect traversing hollow wood
that's something, at least, we know how to propagate with words

infusing the minuscule
into paper
that was
bark and fiber, and that becomes our unforeseeable tree.

RED-HOT

Petty thief
I steal
apples
to counter death

I pile them in front of the window
polish them till they glow, tell myself

I want to be
this decoy orchard
that the sun stokes red-hot.

In the woods leaves
pause at the tree line
in the clearing a tall upright stone
resembles a woman
not entirely formed
who might have been hauled up from underground

I
want
nothing more she says
than to be a piece
of this earth that skimped on me

don't give me a heart, its warped beat
barely audible,

let lightning strike open the soil
slide me back into underbrush
return me to the indistinct.

And we abandoned her among the leaves,
unable
to make death die.

If we speak in fables, it's just
like thick grass protecting
fruit as it falls
from bruising.

After having followed the formidable path, I will be
weighed by the god

I will say "I did not" according to the ritual:

I did not bring into the world
additional uncertainty

I did not
injure anyone
against life's blind wall

I did not
love my own birth
but
taking stock of my life
I
did not
find it lacking.

My acts will be pardoned by the god
that is the How of darkness.

I hang my life
on clothes hangers

they misshape it

too curved
too small

at least I don't leave it in a heap
my life, which is getting old
and looks for proof
that we live here.

What is this face
reflected in the depths of village washhouses
with no woman kneeling beside the water?

What is this face that's trembling
if not the memory of so many women washing?

Left by a bird's beak, by the wind,
we also see petals on the surface

but the face, with its wet smile,
comes from other depths of time

it's the same with cracks in certain stones,
or a faint animal odor
in an abandoned pasture.

What drives you
into the half-open gap in things?

What makes you concentrate on a name?

—The possibility of a world
in which time
both null and rent
would be just
an interval of words in space.

Black the water
over small bones of beasts
and
rotting leaves

smell black, but the water
doesn't smell at all

goes deep into the lungs
from the ditch

it enters through the mouth
and leaves
through the genitals

yes, and the bones of beasts
move a little
now
inside our own.

The throat awakens full of dirt,
having eaten the dead
so long expelled from memory.

All day it tries
to spit them out
until the evening meal
when a plate reveals a crack
that opened long ago under the glaze

break
shatter
toss it out.

Some relief:

with the pieces

the dead pretend to sink to the bottom of the trash.

When evening comes
I light my fingernails

furiously
I ask Who
for a little What

anything at all
not the moon
just a chance, a shadow.

Nothing.

Then I cut my left wrist
set it into a candelabra

with its five lights, I write.

Cut the round loaf, villager,
for the penetrating scent
of each slice

also cut into
the shared tongue
a poem
for the depths of the body.

Hearing
the city drone.

A very harsh melody
insistent
wailing
with flashes of joy.

Up comes the wind
to sweep away the noise.

It smells like a wet dog
because it followed all the funeral processions for dead souls.

Its barking celebrates
a kind of innocence
rising from things gone generally astray.

September, eleven o'clock in the morning, without you.

Everything's pretending
cars in the street
small creatures, spiders, insects on the balcony.

The key turns, the eggs break.

It's even possible to think about Ulysses, the Talmud, Venice.

The truth, however, is that I'm standing
on a very approximate edge of things.

Replanting the hellebore
I talk to myself
about feeding the cosmos:
nothing but that

a spoonful of earth
for the root that's still visible

a spoonful
to top off the pot

one
for the entire planet

the last one
for its vertical rise toward the enigma.

I desire you in our time
which is now well on in years.

Seasons, troubles,
human misfortunes, our misfortunes

traversing them
throughout.

We did not renounce the form of hours.

It's really you, dear body, dear words.
It's really the world,
lost as ever in madness.

We grew old
each day divorcing
our faces of the day before

little by little countries made friends with us
we deciphered ancient writings on stones

the world grew
more tenderly
round

it took its time
lending the stone and the moon to us
and leading us toward
a dreamlike overabundance.

Worried about
the body, the earth,
I examine little nothings.

Hardly exist.

Don't exist?

zero matter
compared to the What
that we don't know at all, except
that it's something else, unfathomable.

But the red of a red radish
shadows through crimson curtains in the lovers' chamber,
do they proclaim any less
radiance, mystery?

I take their pulse
I record their fables, I add them
to the ancient accounts, inhabiting insatiable absence
through these luminosities that reach
as far as the constellations.

I remain
the faithful liege
of nothings.

Twenty or thirty centuries ago

a poet my brother
was watching a tiny insect
walking the length of his arm.

He was struck with amazement
at being there, in the world, both of them at the same time
in a shared fold among the vast
combinations of the universe.

Attacks, wars, suns gone berserk,
not far away cities were burning.

By chance spared, by chance together,

between the lines
of the inexorable

the poet and the insect endured.

It's sad
around you?

It's already dying?

Listen to your pleura sing a little
with the wind,
leafing through the tree, become its friend,
consider yourself a paraphrase of autumn.

If this vital operation
is successful,
you'll no longer be a stranger to seeds.

Scent of linden trees
their pollen in rain.

I inhabit the visible

by that, I will never be deserted

under the trees
stones and beetles
are enough for my geography

my vertical green
the night under my feet:
ecumenical landscape.

Where on earth, it doesn't matter
it's here, in the moment,
beginning and end.

At day's end things join up

flowers and cat, book and lamp,
dreaming of primordial magma,

approach our borders
where we admit them so absentmindedly.

Nevertheless, identifying our realm
might be the evening's most urgent business.

Under the curses of birds
a few men wander among stones

some of which evoke an ancient arch
a Gothic church
or a square
guarded by a tower

others are scattered, but cut with care.

That might be moonlight
if it didn't come from many points in the sky.

There is much
of the elsewhere in this scene of distorted time
that often presents itself to me.

Let's say, to a *slightly elsewhere of me.*

—What did you say? Lost empires,
old age,
indecipherable writing, catastrophes?

—And me? At the present moment, it's this piece of soap
I care about.

I'm holding on to it
white, solid without being hard.

Many other bars of soap wore away,
softened, grew thinner in my hands.

Now,
six forty-seven a.m., in July,
I'm clutching this piece

thanks to it I feel alive
despite earthquakes and the fall of Babylon.

Writing?

Yes, to elicit the presence
of all lives
especially the very slight

starfish
ant on a burdock leaf

and the leaf itself.

Slowly, little by little, life
emerges into the positive
and suffices.

Unannotated.

Little breaths, the moments of our lives.

No doubt
afterward merged
with a cosmic breathing?

But that long exhale of the universe
is too distant
for us

imposed
by whom, why,
stranger to the sweetnesses we share.

Archaeologists of the sky, sometimes we think we detect it in a miraculously silent lane, cutting through the tourists and car horns of a foreign city.

Sometimes.

And then, nothing more. Gone.

Our presence
sometimes
becomes strange to us

as though it left us to start down some path
centaur
with no rider?

—At least not looking back

afraid
of the monstrous landscapes
behind us

or that the earth
with hardly a sound
might drain away
into nothingness.

Our lungs breathe,
our blood circulates, our digestive system functions.

Any chance of restful sleep?

—Not likely!
Crazy images flash past

one adventure
exclaiming over another.

Erratic blossoms
occupy your brain.

Also asleep, the cat beside us sighs and stretches its claws.

All three of us are traversing matter's complicated dreams.

The decorum of words

the poets go about
stripping it clean

that's their job
sanitation workers, demolishers
down to naked matter
and sign, password:

desire
desert

everything

sometimes it's slaughter

The patient in the recovery room
sees white.

Everything
is both possible and far away

the sky
fluffy with clouds

words
all the same
a little empty.

Even one's love feels weightless

and thinking of one's life, its rather useless days
all mixed up
with pale recovery-room curtains.

The poor stone I'm holding
makes up part
of a shared existence

it has rights to the cliff

it's sufficient for naming
everything rough, everything hard in this world
and it seizes control
in the hollow of my hand
extended as though in greeting.

Very dark matter
works in me when I write
like bread dough
rolled in the hands of unknown
illiterate women
who before me mixed kneaded loaded the ovens
followed obscure rituals to accompany their baking.

I sense a shared community with them.

Nevertheless, in their bread making
I must break with them,
transferring to words the site of this burning
attention to such essential details
the need to put the body
in contact
with the world.

Hello goodbye you others from before,

women of the north with hands covered in flour
women of the south slowly peeling chestnuts!

At that time, to represent an absurdity or strong emotion,
painters made portraits of imaginary characters,
which were called *tronies*.

Rembrandt made one of himself as the tronie:

Self-portrait with an open mouth.

It's of someone in pain.

But what kind of pain?
Toothache, the pain of being abandoned, worry,
terrible metaphysical pain?

Yes, all that at once maybe: the pain of being, in body
and in soul.

Anguish
over the moment that will follow.

Mouth opening into a cry
that's addressed to humanity down through the centuries

and that won't receive a response.

Yes, heavy, the blood
designs
networks on the skin

pulses in the neck

death is swimming there
a little more persuasive each day
carrying rot along with it
before tossing the body onto the sidewalk beyond time.

Meanwhile, waking suddenly at night,
they remember
then stitch up sleep around their lives again.

The mirror retains
on its surface the *is this really me*
who feels time in my blood
who thinks daily of the day deducted
from a total
unknown to me?

I turn my back to it
pigheaded I still choose
to reject that question
in favor of the visible.

Into my spinal column
I withdraw

I inhabit it
bone by bone

infinitely alone and vulnerable

but sometimes
it's truly beautiful
it's a second recuperation
in a life of grass between stones

To be traversed
by whatever is most ripe in the world: fruit, poem

or simply
to cash in that dream for small change.

One's finger traces the arc a drop of brandy leaves on the table

outside
the icy road.

A warm and fleeting taste
fills the mouth, infuses the whole body.

Tremble
that's the name
for aspen, their furtive shimmer.

Leaves flash

their life scintillates

instant after instant
they whisper
that we too have sparkling moments
tiny, gleaming traces of us on earth.

As for me, I inhabited a large bird.
Its warm entrails nestled me.
I fed on its developing eggs.

Suddenly, I was the one
that it laid in the cold light.
I inhabit the few years left to me.

Strict immanence is my mother
and graffiti on earth or water:

legs of flaming pink
corners of the mountain.

How many trees in the course of this journey
rose to speak between us and the sky
and we didn't know their names

any more
than the names of insects under their bark, among their leaves.

But quiet labor came of this anonymity

each element hardly mattered

we lived like filigree
within their enigmatic whole

In our turn
we were
evident
and inexplicable

That trembling
goes far
out to sea

effect of the light?
huge flock of birds escaping?

To counter doubt
one sets
close by
the pot of orange flowers

the *here and now*
to block the view.

I'm endlessly obsessed with one desire:
to show the world a part of my body
that we think about so little
it seems almost indecent to look at it

that is, the spleen
the size of a fist

yes, to display it
a red so close to infrared
it turns black

maybe it would stop straying off then

it would attract a crowd.

And me
brandishing that black sponge
I would stop living on the periphery of my flesh

I'd make a great sales pitch for it, every day.

Briefly
we will have traveled through life

the alphabet
aloe rubbed onto fingers and fingernails
so children won't suck them

then books
their scent of old ink
hasn't left us. We loved the smell of them
like skin

one day
we'll no longer bring our hands to our nostrils
to sniff our own skin

life leaves us a little each day, we no longer
even run
after it.

Briefly we will have traveled through it
toward that other destiny where we'll merge
with unknown cells, perhaps with scents we never imagined,
travelers from being to being: wheat, dog, pebble,
    magnificent cities.

Each thing according to
its emergence into a form of life

Each life according to
roles fashioned
slowly
rituals of the species.

And if I dream of an elsewhere, the cat
as I stroke her offers me an infinite journey
splayed like the most innocent
courtesan, belly up, paws every which way

outside the window, a bumblebee
dives into a primrose, in raptures
its antennae coated with pollen, then flies off
black and glistening like the cat.

*Their lives I cannot penetrate, but I share with them a place
on earth, a very brief moment in the millennia. They are. They
receive the world, keep the promises of their lives.*

What else do I do?

On window panes, curtains, books, camp the invisible.

Tiny bodies and claws. Desires, dislikes.
Sometimes they engage in battle, sometimes they mate or
    schedule friendly meetings.
They cling, caress.

In my study, where they mob, I celebrate a blind tranquility.

. . . At the border of the inexorable
we are still
on living earth

we have not *crossed over*.

Almost

but life's brightly colored
hachures still traverse us

with morning coffee
we sign the pact of the living

even
the cup overflows a little on our fingers
because that alliance
is without bounds.

No, I will not swallow
your phantom words
your inventory charts, your graphs
for stock markets, massacres.

I choose the cries
of seabirds

the creaking of stones

everything that defies, screams, explodes mutely in the world.

Blood at the temples, beating heart, tick of the arteries,
this is my word as well
palpable under the fingertips.

If I could seize a *little nothing*
a bit of *nothing*
all things would come to me
those that dance
in its cloth. ·

If I could
bite into things in their fullness
I would know the deep taste of the world

indecisive
I stand up straight at least

between my lips
the beginning of an anthem
to melt snow
to sound rhythms across the earth . . .

Time can be heard beating
like a promise of life inside an egg.

Yes, I sank
not all the way to the bottom
but into total absence.

Anonymous walls.
Yellow sheets marked "Public Assistance."
They told me nothing: I still knew how to spell, but not how
to read.

People all around annoyed me, large tormenting insects, too
lively.
Under my tube-fed skin
they went to work: tubes, injections . . .

I was learning that death wasn't easy.

I came back to life. Oh, monorail world, transport me
a little longer,
successive
darknesses and daylights!

Don't descend
any deeper
than pain

it levels off in places where you can rest

sometimes it reveals a tiny part of the body, unknown
to you till then

but any lower
and it's beyond your grasp.

You'll be trapped in the hollow
of a huge bell
you'll be
flattened
quashed.

Watch out.

There are bruised words
outside the door

don't open it

they're all piled up, there'd be chaos
some are still climbing the stairs

Maybe
they're coming for
silence. Their silence.

If you opened the door
they'd enter the dictionaries

they'd occupy those calm dwellings
of alphabetical order, where nothing proves
that horror actually exists

but blood
would flow from them
each time we came to the word "blood."

Strange, the objects in certain categories
carefully filed away, of little use
just short of useless
with some kind of terrible beauty.

Pill bottles, potato peelers ...

It's as if they were asking us to explain their loneliness, as
compared to the knife, the pills. As if they attributed to some
god of the superfluous our equally futile presence. Yet there
they are, tenacious, hardly but truly useful.
Maybe like us.

You know what it means
to be sick.

But to be sick in the body
or in the head?

It's all blurry like smudged patterns on tiles
or the trace of lipstick on a cheek

blurred
crossed out even

we suffer
body and soul

just like at other times when joy
inundates our arteries and toenails.

Can we
delight or sadden stone?

With our attention so partial
to the living
what are we in the face of the apparently inert?

—Palm against an old wall
we thought we were only touching the insensible.
The mineral grows warm under our flesh,
germinates a barely perceptible
existence of tiny mosses, furtive insects.

A muted call to share
a secret life
reaches us from the depths of time:
the stone exudes a bit of moisture, like a tear.

. . . how tenuous the darkness, sometimes.

Inhale the strong odor of the streets.
Touch the space
between speech and death.

One day, it will close up in your hand.

Our sad, neutral name will remain,
plus maybe the memory
of a moment you loved

. . . when you pressed your face
against another's
or the bright red wound of a tree. . .

Today your blood pulses.
You have only to touch your wrist
to bear your life, passionately.

We don't want
to pay full price for your catalog of worries
to shoulder the loss of the gods
to lower our voices over newspaper headlines, conspiracies.

We refuse passage on the vast ship
bound for shipwreck.

We are withdrawing into our domain,
narrow—it's true—
like the sides of Jonah's whale
but livable:
capitulation of thistle
closed
around a bee.

Against my cheek
the sunbathed door of the armoire.

Encounter of flesh and wood
in the heat.

What a mad morning caress,

how absolute
a moment!

"See you shortly, in the unknown,"
nothing mysterious about that appointment.

But such certainty is no more
reassuring
than the huge flights of birds
rising over the trees.

Someone is weeping below them.

In autumn, life hurries on.

Growing paler and paler
the hands
that embrace the scaly trunks.

To the heights of incandescence
of timelessness
my poetry doesn't aspire

what extreme would gratify me?
if my words could disappear
into matter, itself
perked up, revived,
having welcomed them into its mystery.

When do you want to divorce yourself?
—When I've completely lost
the names of my friends, smiling in photographs,
an arm around my shoulder.

Life leaves us bit by bit

first our memory fills up with *in memoriam*s
then it fails and we forget our very selves.

That fog
stretches as far as the great elsewhere.

When I think of you, I transform into tree-lined paths
very leafy urban landscape seen from the room where
I'm standing.
A minuscule realm
with its special hour, the beauty of its laws
                            that are ineffectual,
and its guardian bird, who never rests,
who watches and watches
to keep death from having our eyes.

I don't believe in heaven
as the dwelling place of the blessed

blessed am I
shaken
moment after moment
by a caressed animal
by your glimpsed profile

I name, I touch
these visible pleasures

elsewhere is nil
elsewhere is not

Nevertheless its cold hand
will close around me.
I won't even be able
to blame it
for the enormous malice of the universe.

To approach a word
Like a body
Very gently
Then
In the heat of possession

Every minute is first, when the garden
shares its light with the silence

just passing through time like us
the dog near the greenery
plays ambassador
extending to us a front paw
back paws
in the shade of the leaves.

moment of exchange

sap
blood
drop of water.

As though
in a hole in time
a silence settled
that could be heard in the heart of the city

in the heart
of its whistling station, its market.

That would transport us to the outskirts of memory:
forest of the long, long ago
soothing sleep beside an abandoned canal.

Words would shed their meanings
they would become
a taste on the tongue
the unformulated of our deep body.

As though
in a hole in time
we heard
a secret
nearly inaudible
regarding the why of our life.

Return the love of the least things
so disdained by us,
old snow, worn paper.

You'll feel the remanence of days
you'll bond with departed faces
you'll consider yourself in a different light.

For the music of stones
you have to wait a long time

motionless
between the ground and the morning sky
we feel the fresh force of the sun
making the earth vibrate

mosaic of sounds

then we stretch out beside pebbles.

In closest proximity
our bodies share
the brief respite of the universe.

—And nevertheless I pressed against your face my own.
And nevertheless that was
filled with joy like an inlet during seaside holidays

and nevertheless that was
sometimes tortured like certain dead wood.

That was. Very much so.

You've got a run in your peritoneum
there's a dog barking in your femur
and you think you can write a pastoral?

Eclogue country, ha! So much for
the hunted prey
so much for
the baby abandoned on the trash heap.

Existence! You're going to accompany all that with flutes?
Brute that you are, you have
something else to cry

something dissonant.

Sitting in the park
by the sandpile
meant for children
the old man thinks of the dead

his heart is dried up, so close to his own death

he resembles the sand
gradually swallowed by the earth, and replaceable.

But when he walks in the garden
he heads toward the center
of a particular time

that of a tree

and when his hand closes
around one of the tree's fruits
he attains the center of the center: a bond
with the whole of life, and reversible time.

Collect a seed
place it in the center
of your palm.

from the balcony high above the city, give it a chance

gently blow it away.

On the breeze coming from the river
it will be carried in the direction of a forest

in twenty years an unexpected tree
will bear witness
that a woman, also born by chance,
released to its fate this tiny scrap of universe.

We're always holding the end of the world, no matter where.

It doesn't refuse
to be broken like fresh bread.

A very ripe apricot gets smashed
on the path. Food for small creatures.

The horse passing
delicately curls its lips
around the end of a branch, eats
fruit after fruit with a faint sound.

For me?
—The odor
and the idea that
the entire world
might remain light ocher, sweet summer, bee.

Pain: explosion, spasms.

The back of the throat
reveals itself as animal flesh,
wet and throbbing.

It's brutal, what attaches us most to being.

In extremity we revert to
primordial soup, where cells vaguely quiver.

What did you do, if not
walk this firebrand earth

searching for a place

but the journey was endless.

Searching for someone. But who
would go searching without taking someone's hand.

Even the ends of branches
could have been your country.

Lost, you took off with the galaxy
but you cling to a word that stayed with you, heard by
chance in a doorway like a solitary horse receives a caress.

A word
become
sun and place.

I'm writing a letter to I don't know whom
a letter to send I don't know where.

I'm announcing that in autumn
the branches must not be ignored
magnificently playing their score for brass.

Such important news, in the midst of wars,
catastrophes,
to let it be known.

On the envelope:
For X, in whatever sad country.

In my body there's
something to write
on the sleek membranes of the intestines
something to quench thirst
by opening a small vein or two
something for sleep
in the lungs' alveoli

there's something raw
something dirty
and maybe some walks to take, with a miner's lamp,
along the arm and leg bones

what my body wants is to glide all by itself
on the rivers of air, the currents
that carry balloons and sailplanes

never will it be Icarus or a bird

never will I be its definitive
subterranean
adventurer.

Holes in the bark

the deep eyes of trees
visible when leaves come down in autumn
bore into you at night.

However much you pull the sheets over your head
they penetrate your eye sockets, enter your body
descend
through the shafts of bones, the circulatory system
to collect your living confession
that dreams, snorts, guzzles
at the surface
but can't get its bearings in the dark of your flesh.

Oh, those eyes, eyes of Osiris, the great judge,
scattered about the forest!
Morning walker,
you have unknowingly summoned them into your depths.

Every morning I form
one body with my body
surprised to find it there, contradictory

The old woman said to Phaedra:
We love this existence
because no one has ever returned
bringing news from any other.

But also we love it because sometimes
the light is riotous in the sky
and oranges are sweet in the back of the throat.

So we accept gravity and quanta
multiplication tables and imaginary numbers
matter and antimatter.

Don't wake me sleeper
with that instinctive movement
of your shoulder

don't wake me it's my insides that recognize you

even the most naked pleasure
is less perfect
than the passions of shadowy things in my body.

Small noise, rain.

Ant cavalry
on thin legs whispers in leaves.

The afternoon is not prophetic
but like so many others.

We like its simplicity.

In the windows our faces are inscribed
a little blurry
as if we wanted to steal the landscape
and transport it for good into our house.

It would let us live in it, uneventfully.

We would be strategists of raindrops and twigs,

we would preserve the peace.

Following the edge of an island
into a field
that reminded us of Corfu?

—But decidedly land, the grass
with only its own scent, far from the sea.

Our memory so vivid, it's the sun that gives rise to it
and your hand in mine, and the great space breathing.

Hours turn in the humus.

Everything passes and reappears and breathes
like an animal
its life
deeper
than all memory.

... But so far off, so unrealized, the peace I'm seeking!

How can I embrace the clouds,
touch the sky's flesh,

since
I've come to such a sorry end
with earth

with my explorations and my worries ...

New world?

It was the day of the first cavalry,
arising suddenly all on horseback,
with no previous warning,
soldiers by the thousands.

The sky
suddenly
shed its strange petals,

and with that, horses' legs
manes
riders
fell like rain. Straight down.

The world order exchanged centuries,
the twenty-first for the eighteenth,

leaving us perplexed by this renewal gone awry, that no party
had written into its program.

But there were still wars and massacres.

Very quickly we adapted.

End-of-life accompanist,

I didn't invent that description.

It appeared in a book, following a poem, as its author might
note an occupation, a pursuit, or, more accurately, a pastime,
which
in this case
would absolutely deserve that name . . . ("passing time,
killing time . . .")

Getting past a lifetime, like getting over a vice, a desire!

—Come on now, it wasn't so great, this existence,
let's do an inventory, fold it up, put it carefully away . . .

For the next episode, see solutions of all kinds: paradise,
oblivion, another incarnation, eternal memory, so many
choices!

The essential thing is seeing life through
to the end. Like difficult schooling.

It's possible/impossible
to go into reclusion
alone with one's life
stripped naked, vowed to silence.

A very small insect on the wall
clambers madly
toward
even tinier prey.

Through the window
a pigeon sings

its cooing is always the same
like a biography without adventure,
except today: abrupt stop, then
two new notes, ah, that disconcerting conclusion . . .

—And suddenly the room
becomes a bustling crossroads, full of drama.

With your chagrin, you meant to stay alone,

taking time for phrasings, for retrospective accounts.

But no, your chagrin surrounds you,
it sticks to your papers, it soils your fingers,

it even
sits down at the table with friends.

Everything
has suddenly gotten old and faded, good for the scrap heap.

We are a little bit of grass suddenly uprooted in the nothingness.

and we forget to be
as is mandatory
for all of us
"someone cheerful."

It's as if there were an earth above
just beyond the clouds
so transparent that our eyes couldn't see it.

Our doubles
not very high up
live our lives, but in total malevolence,
pale, reunited, each night.
Imitating us, but much more grotesque.

We will never meet them.

Nevertheless we suspect them, sometimes.

. . . But what if it were absurd, our turmoil?

If it came
from a question infinitely misframed?

All our studies, our definitions, studded with wounds . . .

Ah, in a box of secrets
yes, the word that would reunite
the seed and the forest, the "forever" and the passing!

Sick.
Caught, beaten, crushed,
bitten into,
gnawed beneath the skin,
prey of what predators?

—Yes, we know, we know
that they chew very delicately on what's most sensitive.

Nothing more?
— ... We still have to
congratulate ourselves on being able to feel something.

... Because we're not dead yet.
—Maybe that's
just asking for trouble?

Then a scene imposes itself upon you, impossibly banal: a man in yellow overalls hoses down the sidewalk.
And suddenly, you taste the sharp flavor of existence.

She doesn't have a name.
She has all of them.

She brings to mind the unknown.

She has that definitive voice
we attribute to stuffed animals, to dolls.

She is that dream of happiness
that presupposes a childhood.

In short: she doesn't exist.
. . . But we invent her.

How I searched for you, life,
in beings with blood and bark
in the elephant's great mouth
in the centipede's scrap of flesh!

Sometimes, life,
you pulsed in the inexplicable gaze of a creature,
but never
did you
choose me, love me, spontaneously.

. . . Or else, was it me who rejected your advances?

Why this feeling of exile
that returns regularly
even though love and friendship
are so close by.
No doubt it's the childhood I missed, illness
always at hand.
And yet love, friendship are here, right next to me.
But I feel, I don't know, some need for "more,"
more "positivity,"
impossible, surely.

A very large white pigeon
inside our balcony
every day at twelve-thirty,
what does he come looking for?
No female pigeon around here,
no food either.
He flies off after perching
on a big cluster of blue flowers.
Maybe he's dreaming of a sea
that same color,
that he might have known in his youth, then abandoned
for our civilization,
where, on his own, he lives on dreams
formed of memories.

These are my "Sorrows" I'm writing,
not those of the banishment and exile imposed
on Ovid,
but those of the suffering body that often knows
the exile of a bed it's not allowed to leave.

So soft, the gray of the sky sometimes occupied by white clouds, that one would like to be a bird to take pleasure in it. Soon it will be night. It will be the hour of secret birds, the book sought in the library, and finally sleep, half see-through, half seeing-eye dog. Thanks to which, we will reign over the flowers, night, and the world, as multiple sovereigns, obscure and fragile.

Nevertheless love
conforms to love.
There is no bird couple that doesn't resemble us.
And from their rooftop, they watch us
with a kind of radiance,
they evoke a time when animals spoke,
when animals and birds spoke together,
while humans, now so talkative,
kept quiet.
We might have to learn the world through their chirps
so confidential at present
that we can't decipher them.
We would remain seated under their trees,
and listen to them like children
listen to the teacher.
Our silence,
and the steadiness of their chirping
would help us live.

As if the earth
gently spread
its tiredness
over ours
and illness once declared
was filled with tirednesses,
leaves separated from branches,
lake difficult to drink.
And we caress it like a creature
who could be our sister,
but there she is rejecting us,
because we are not of her race.
And it's in vain that humans stroke earth,
in vain that they write "earth."
We would need to know everything
according to the dimensions
that earth guards within its grandeur.

In a little while, I will no longer be, you will no longer be.
The real sorrow is that day by day that day approaches, and
what persists is our ignorance with regard to it.
Tomorrow, or in a week, a month . . .
And under the earth of unbelievers only silence reigns, or
maybe the cracking sound of what was a tiny creature.
—But the "will no longer be" conceals nothing, because in
no language, it seems to me, does that sound exist.
Oh, hold me as long as you can, musician. You filled with
caresses my existence that is going.

Tout à l'heure, je ne
serai plus, tu ne seras plus.
La vraie douleur, c'est que
de jour en jour ce jour appro-
che,
mais ce qui persiste, c'est ton
ignorance à son propos. Demain
ou dans une semaine, un mois....
Et sous la terre des in-
croyants, ne règne que ce
silence, ou peut-être le bruit
d'une brisure par tel petit
animal minuscule sur ce ... il
— Mais ce "n'y sens plus"
ne mange rien, car dans sa ...
langue, me semble-t-il, ce bruit
n'existe. Ah, sens-moi tant
que tu peux, musicien. Tu as tort
de caresser ... stence puis en va

NOTES

All the poems in this collection were translated from the French versions as they appear in *Toute minute est première* by Marie-Claire Bancquart, preface by Claude Ber, published by Le Castor Astral, 2019. The titles of the original volumes, from which all but the final seven unpublished poems were drawn, are as follows:

Avec la mort, quartier d'orange entre les dents (2005)
Verticale du secret (2007)
Terre énergumène (2009)
Violente vie (2012)
Mots de passe (2014)
Qui vient de loin (2016)
Tracé du vivant (2017)
Figures de la terres (2017)

MARIE-CLAIRE BANCQUART (1932–2019) is a major French poet. The author of novels, essays, and literary criticism as well, she wrote more than twenty volumes of poetry for which she received numerous prizes, including the Paul Verlaine Prize from the Académie française. With her husband, the musician and composer Alain Bancquart, she lived in Paris for most of her life and taught French literature at the Université Paris-Sorbonne until her retirement in 1994. *Toute minute est première* was published posthumously in France the year of her death.

JODY GLADDING is a poet and translator with five poetry collections, most recently *I entered without words*, and forty translations from French. She has translated works by Roland Barthes, Jean Giono, Julia Kristeva, and Pierre Michon. Her awards include the French-American Foundation Translation Prize, the Yale Series of Younger Poets prize, and the Whiting Award. She lives and works in East Calais, Vermont.

milkweed
EDITIONS

Founded as a nonprofit organization in 1980, Milkweed Editions is an independent publisher. Our mission is to identify, nurture, and publish transformative literature, and build an engaged community around it.

Milkweed Editions is based in Bdé Óta Othúŋwe (Minneapolis) within Mní Sota Makhóčhe, the traditional homeland of the Dakhóta people. Residing here since time immemorial, Dakhóta people still call Mní Sota Makhóčhe home, with four federally recognized Dakhóta nations and many more Dakhóta people residing in what is now the state of Minnesota. Due to continued legacies of colonization, genocide, and forced removal, generations of Dakhóta people remain disenfranchised from their traditional homeland. Presently, Mní Sota Makhočhe has become a refuge and home for many Indigenous nations and peoples, including seven federally recognized Ojibwe nations. We humbly encourage our readers to reflect upon the historical legacies held in the lands they occupy.

milkweed.org

Milkweed Editions, an independent nonprofit literary publisher, gratefully acknowledges sustaining support from our board of directors, the McKnight Foundation, the National Endowment for the Arts, and many generous contributions from foundations, corporations, and thousands of individuals—our readers.

This activity is made possible by the voters of Minnesota through a Minnesota State Arts Board Operating Support grant, thanks to a legislative appropriation from the arts and cultural heritage fund.

Interior design by Mary Austin Speaker
Typeset in PS Fournier

Fournier is a typeface created by the Monotype
Corporation in 1924, based on types cut in the mid-
eighteenth century by Pierre-Simon Fournier, a French
typographer. The specific cuts used as a reference for
Fournier are referred to as "St Augustin Ordinaire" in
Fournier's influential *Manuel typographique*,
published in 1764 in Paris.